Serving soup from a Derby porcelain tureen, about 1790. Soup was eaten with the table spoon.

TABLE SETTINGS

Robin Emmerson

Shire Publications Ltd

CONTENTS

Printed in Great Britain by C. I. Thomas & Sons (Haverfordwest) Ltd, Press Buildings, Merlins Bridge, Haverfordwest, Dyfed SA61 1XF.

British Library Cataloguing in Publication Data: Emmerson, Robin. Table settings. I. Title. 642.6. ISBN 0-7478-0139-8.

ACKNOWLEDGEMENTS
Photographs are acknowledged as follows: British Library, page 19; Broadfield House Glass Museum, Kingswinford, pages 27 and 28; Anna de Soissons, page 22 (centre). For the drawings I am grateful to my wife June. I am grateful to the Norfolk Museums Service for the opportunity to study the collections in its care, and to a private owner for kindly allowing access to pieces in the family collection.

Cover: *An eighteenth-century recipe for 'ribbon jelly' served on a pyramid of glass salvers.*

Below left: *The language of hospitality. Since a cover on a cup showed respect, it was emphasised with decoration. A steeple cup, silver-gilt, 1617.*

Below right: *A ceremonial great salt. The part which held salt, a shallow dish above the drum and below the cover, is very small. Silver-gilt, 1568, Norwich Guildhall.*

A porringer with a cover. One could drink from it or eat from it with a spoon. Silver, 1656.

THE SEVENTEENTH CENTURY

In 1665 Robert May suggested the perfect spectacle for a dinner table: a pie containing live frogs and another full of live birds; a galleon and a castle, complete with guns, and a stag with an arrow in its side, all made of confectioner's paste. The guns have trains of real gunpowder and the stag is full of claret:

'Being all placed in order upon the Table, before you fire the trains of powder, order it so that some of the Ladies may be persuaded to pluck the Arrow out of the Stag, then will the Claret wine follow as blood running out of a wound. This being done with admiration to the beholders, after some short pause, fire the train of the Castle, that the pieces [guns] all of one side may go off; then fire the trains of one side of the Ship as in a battle ... to sweeten the stink of the powder, let the ladies take the [blown] egg shells full of sweet waters, and throw them at each other. All dangers being seemingly over, by this time you may

suppose they will desire to see what is in the pies; where lifting first the lid of one pie, out skips some Frogs, which makes the Ladies to skip and shriek; next after the other pie, whence comes out the birds; who by a natural instinct flying at the light, will put out the candles: so that what with the flying birds, and skipping frogs, the one above, the other beneath, will cause much delight and pleasure to the whole company.'

Such spectacles were then old-fashioned, belonging to a medieval tradition of impressing the eyes rather than the palate. A heron made a noble dish because it was a noble bird, certainly not because of its taste, which was unpleasantly fishy. The visual splendour of a feast expressed the status of the host and of the occasion. This inherited medieval ceremony has left one or two relics to this day. The reason why cups for sports presentations sometimes have covers is ultimately because a covered cup at a

3

Left: *The answer to sticky fingers. A ewer, fitted over the boss in the centre of its basin, to enable a servant to carry them together. Silver-gilt, 1617, Norwich Guildhall.*

Right: *A posset pot, about 1700. It has two spouts for sucking, which run down inside two of the four handles. The tip of one spout is missing.*

medieval feast indicated that its user was one of the most important people present. It became normal that any drinking cup offered as a mark of special favour should have a cover. The flamboyant decoration often applied to covers was a visible gesture of respect to one's guests, a reassuring token of a worthy and hospitable welcome. The cover may even have retained some practical advantage in an age when etiquette books were still advising their readers that, if they must spit, they should not do it across the table.

The ceremonial salt pot of medieval tradition retained much of its importance in early Stuart times. Its great size, out of all proportion to its tiny pan for salt, was intended to mark out the most important person at the table. The phrase 'below the salt' is still in use to indicate inferior position.

Forks did not come into general use until late in the century. Food was divided into what could be handled with the fingers and what needed a spoon: 'spoon-meat' as it was called. In the absence of forks, it was easiest to eat meat with a spoon in the

A buffet in operation at the coronation banquet of William and Mary, 1688. Many buffets served more to show off the silver than to assist the diners.

4

liquid it was cooked in. This was usually thickened with cereals. (Potatoes did not replace cereals as the normal accompaniment for meat until the eighteenth century.) The deep bowls known generally as porringers, with one or two handles, were ideal for such mixtures, because they did not restrict one to using one's spoon. *The Compleat Cook* of 1655 advises of a Spanish olio (a dish of fowl and flesh served with the liquid in which it was cooked) that 'the Broth is rather to be drunk out of a Porringer, than to be eaten with a spoon'.

Before the 1660s one did not necessarily expect to find a set of spoons laid ready on the table when one went out to dinner. One tended to carry one's own spoon, which made it an important personal possession. If you owned one piece of silver, it was a spoon. A child was therefore born with a silver spoon in its mouth, or, if not, that was the perfect christening present. After the Restoration the table spoon was adopted from France. The name itself indicates that previously spoons were not generally laid on the table ready for use, and the term has survived into modern speech.

When diners ate without forks, their fingers became sticky. Servants would carry around the table a ewer or water jug and a basin. The water, often scented with rose petals, was poured over a diner's hands and caught in the basin held beneath them.

When not in use, ewer and basin would sit on a buffet, the equivalent of the later sideboard, together with drinking cups and the flagons for refilling them. A buffet loaded with silver had been a status symbol since the middle ages, and the number of its steps or tiers for display could express precise distinctions of rank. It was also known quite accurately as a cup-board and, despite the gradual enclosure of its open shelves by doors, we still call its modern descendants cupboards.

Enough large deep pottery cups survive from the seventeenth century to indicate that there was a tradition of sharing a communal cup, which was presumably passed around the table, either until it was empty or until those present were under the table. In the eighteenth century, when glasses had largely replaced pottery cups for alcoholic drink, the tradition of a shared cup survived in the 'constable' glass, an oversized version of a normal wineglass, which was passed around. Many of the great pottery cups of the seventeenth century have three or more handles, to ensure that any recipient would always have a couple of handles to grasp, whichever side of the cup was presented to him. It therefore seems likely that a multitude of handles came to suggest hospitality and good cheer. Like the meaning of covers, this is another part of a lost language of hospitality expressed in pots.

Some cups, both large and small, have a long spout emerging from the vessel at the lowest possible point. The type is known in pottery, glass and silver. These were used for the drinks of posset and syllabub, which typically consisted of cream curdled with wine or ale and were particular favourites in the seventeenth century. The purpose of the spout was to enable the liquid to be drunk right down to the bottom, avoiding the froth or curd on top, which could be eaten with a spoon. It might seem insanitary to modern taste to suck in turn from the same spout as the pot passed around the table, but many large earthenware pots survive, and the rarity of silver ones may be just because they were worth melting down when habits changed.

These little silver dishes, only some 3 inches (75 mm) across, are often erroneously called wine-tasters but they either held sweetmeats or were the original 'saucers' for sauce. About 1650.

A dinner for the Queen, May 29th.

First Corse

- A Haunch of Venison Rost — To Change
- Beef Royal — To Change
- Veal Ragoust, Collops of Venison
- A Green Pease Pottage of Ducklins
- Fine Puddings of sorts
- A Fricasy of Bean
- Squabs in Lettice
- A Pike Rost Carps Stued with Eels and Flounders
- A Patty of Green Geese
- Pullets in Bladders
- A Pasty of Venison Rost
- A Pull=aloon
- A Ragoust of Sweet Breads
- A Fricasy of Rabbets
- A Westphalia Ham Pye &c
- Deer Sowce Dowcets
- A Dish of Perches Blancht
- Piggs Rost de Arlick — To Change
- A Pottage of Chickens where the Ham Pye is — To Change

Second Corse

- Lamb-Stones and Sweet breads, Omlet of Asparagus
- Ducklings Tame Pidgeons Small Chickens
- A Patty of Artichoaks
- Morells and Troufles
- Puffs of Curd
- Pheasants with Eggs Patridges with Green Corn
- Currant Tart in Jelly
- Codling Tart Cream'd
- A Thames Salmon Sowced and Collar'd
- Shamp=inions
- Pease francois
- Cray-fish
- Soles and Smelts
- Rabbets and Leverets young
- Kidney Beans & Suckers fryd

The symmetry of the table. The second course had to be laid while the diners were seated, but the servants could follow the impressions left on the cloth by the first course. (After Charles Carter, 1730.)

6

A silver epergne of the 1780s. The baskets have clear glass liners.

GEORGIAN DINNERS

A modern visitor to England in 1700 would be struck by the mixture of strict formality over rank with table manners which were in other respects primitive. Different dishes on the table would be presented in turn to the host or hostess, who would then offer them to the guests in order of seniority. In 1756 Martha Bradley criticised the effect of this on the guests: 'They were under a 'Constraint, when every thing was to come from the Hand of the Mistress; they did not care to shew they had large Stomachs, or they were ashamed to speak, or they were sorry to give her Trouble; so that half of them did not dine well. Now every one helps himself as he likes, and where he likes,' which was done by 'sending his Plate to the Person that sits near what he likes'. It was taken for granted that servants would be there to carry out the diners' orders and carry their plates to the dish required.

An eighteenth-century dinner was generally in two courses, dessert being regarded as separate from the dinner proper. The whole of each course was laid on the table together. Early in the century the British adopted the French habit of taking soup at the start of the meal, but the soup tureen was laid at one end of the table as part of the first course and replaced by another dish as soon as soup had been served. The two courses, and often the dessert, were expected to contain a matching number of dishes, which was made evident in the symmetrical layout on the table.

Great importance was placed on genteel manners, for they united the growing band of those in polite society and divided them from those outside it. The old way of setting dinner on long tables implied a graded hierarchy and was inappropriate now that polite company cut itself off from its inferiors. In this exclusive atmosphere the

7

The desire for genteel habits replaced brown slipware pottery, like this dish of about 1700, with porcelain and white pottery.

The soup tureen, an eighteenth-century introduction. Lowestoft porcelain, about 1768.

Left: *A set of silver casters for sugar, pepper and mustard, 1721.*

Right: *Grouping the diners' requirements together for their convenience. A cruet set in creamware pottery, about 1780-1800.*

diners enjoyed greater equality. The presence of servants could be made less obtrusive once many of the diners' requirements were within reach on the table, and there was a new emphasis on grouping such items together.

Casters in sets of three were not a new invention: an order of 1689 specified that they were for sugar, pepper and mustard. By 1705 they were sometimes grouped in a frame with a pair of cruet bottles for oil and vinegar. Mustard was at first served in containers of caster shape to match those for sugar and pepper. The mustard caster either had no piercings or they were masked by a solid inner sleeve. The smaller, uncovered type of mustard pot was not generally used until the eighteenth century. During the 1720s the silver 'surtout' or epergne, a centrepiece incorporating branches holding dishes, and often casters and cruets, salts, sauceboats or spice boxes, developed. The elements could be changed so that for the first course the central basin held a hot dish warmed by a spirit burner underneath, while for dessert a silver bas-

ket of fruit replaced the basin, and candles replaced the dishes on the branches. The epergne gradually lost this flexibility and became just a stand for the dessert, often displaying it on the table throughout the two main courses.

The growing refinement in table manners is reflected in the changing shape of spoons. Before about 1760 they were made with the end of the stem bent in the same direction as the hollow of the bowl. It is easier to pick up the stem if it is kept clear of the table by the bent end, and these spoons were designed to be laid with the bowl downwards. After about 1760 the end is bent in the opposite direction, and the spoon is intended to be laid bowl upwards. Contemporaries evidently took this change seriously, for the records of the London goldsmiths Parker and Wakelin show that their noble customers were bringing in their old spoons to have the ends hammered the other way. The placing with bowl downwards had made sense in an age when bits of other people's dinner — or worse — were likely to land in your spoon.

The Man of Manners, an etiquette book of about 1730, found it necessary to remind readers:

'Coughing, yawning or sneezing over the Dishes, should be carefully avoided; I have been oftentimes in pain to see People, not altogether unacquainted with the Rules of good Manners, guilty of this Indecorum.' The change in spoons demonstrated that the host now trusted his guests' table manners, so that they could pick up their spoons and eat without having to turn them over first.

It was not until late in the seventeenth century that the use of forks became general even among the wealthy. The commonest form of eighteenth-century fork has just two tines, thin, sharp and widely spaced. Such a fork was useless for eating small morsels. Faujas de St Fond noted 'the use of steel forks with two prongs. They are changed at every course. With regard to little bits of meat which they cannot take hold of, recourse is had to the knife which is broad and rounded at the extremity.' Perhaps the later prohibition against eating peas with a knife was precisely because this had once been good manners!

Unless it was served in small pieces as 'spoon-meat', meat had hitherto to be handled with the fingers, and this made it difficult to eat large pieces covered in sticky sauces. The fork enabled diners to cope with French-style dishes with sauce. Sauceboats in silver or china became an essential item on the table after about 1720.

Right: *The stems of spoons change direction, to enable them to be placed the other way up on the table. (Below) Before 1760; (above) after 1760.*

Below right: *One could not eat peas with the fork, but one could with the knife. The commonest eighteenth-century forms, here with handles of agateware pottery, c.1750.*

Below: *The earlier form of sauceboat, double-ended and with a handle either side. Silver, 1735.*

Bottom left: *The later form of sauceboat, less likely to spill when tipped backwards. Worcester porcelain, 1755-60.*

Bottom right: *Neo-classical design preferred tureens for sauce. Derby porcelain, about 1790.*

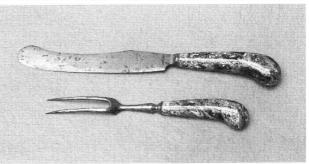

11

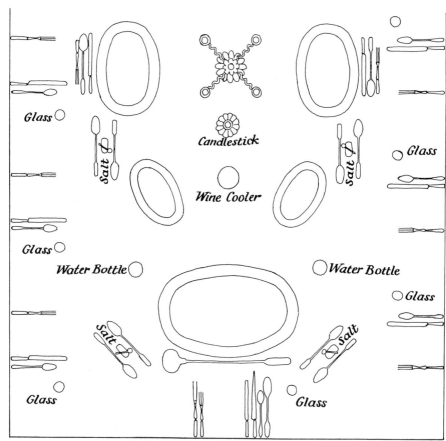

The four-armed epergne marks the centre of a table laid for the first course: the end with the soup is shown. The fish was at the opposite end. (After T. Cosnett, 'The Footman's Director', 1823.)

Once forks were in use, fingers no longer became so sticky, and it was no longer necessary for servants to bring round the ewer and basin to all the diners after each course. Instead, the diners were provided with individual 'wash hand glasses' resembling squat tumblers, each with its own saucer-like stand. They were also made in china. Rochefoucauld in 1784 noted: 'After the sweets you are given water in small bowls of very clear glass in order to rinse out your mouth – a custom which strikes me as extremely unfortunate. The more fashionable do not rinse out their mouths, but that seems to me even worse; for, if you use the water

to wash your hands, it becomes dirty and quite disgusting.'

This is why coloured glass was often used once deep colours became readily available in the later part of the century. By 1800 the bowls were called 'finger-glasses', the change of name no doubt reflecting improved manners. They were required only at the end of the second main course, when butlers were instructed 'to put on those glasses half-full of clean water, when the table is cleared, but before the cloth is removed for dessert'.

Although there is great variety in eighteenth-century drinking glasses, their shapes

12

The soup has been removed and replaced by an entrée. A salt with flanking table spoons was situated at each corner of the table.

An entrée dish of Sheffield plate, the handle on the cover removable so that the cover could double up as an extra dish.

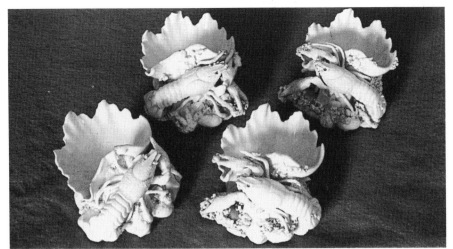

Above: *One for each corner: a set of Chelsea porcelain salts modelled as crayfish, about 1745.*

Below: *Tiny Bow porcelain 'pickle leaves' for individual portions, about 1760.*

Below left: *Wash hand cup, Chelsea porcelain, about 1755. Both the china and the glass versions had stands like saucers.*

Below right: *A 'glass tray' for rinsing and cooling one's wineglass, about 1780 — one way of avoiding being given someone else's dirty glass by a servant.*

14

A Chinese garden made of confectioner's materials, for the centre of the table. (After Gilliers, 1768.)

were not generally varied according to the drinks for which they were intended. Until it became the custom in the nineteenth century to group several glasses by each place setting, there was no need to tell one glass from another. The Georgian diner asked a servant to bring him a glass of a particular wine and, having drunk it, might call for another. The servant removed the empty glass, rinsed it in a cistern at the sideboard, refilled it and brought it back. Swift in his satirical *Directions to Servants* says you can refill one diner's dirty glass for another without bothering to rinse it! Concern about this probably encouraged the use on the table of 'glass trays'. These were bowls

for washing and cooling either one or up to a dozen glasses by hanging them by the foot from notches in the edge, so that the bowls were immersed in iced water. The large versions were sometimes called monteiths.

During dinner it was polite to drink wine only with another person. One diner invited another to drink a glass of wine with him and, once both glasses of wine had been brought, they caught each other's eye, nodded solemnly and simultaneously drained their glasses. Since it was polite to drink with all the other guests, and rude to refuse when asked, eighteenth-century wineglasses needed to have small bowls.

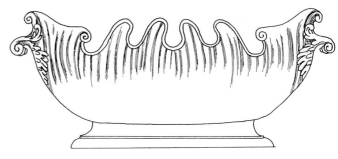

Right: A 'glass tray' or monteith for many glasses. (After the Leeds Pottery catalogue, 1783.)

A few Georgian glasses were made for particular uses: tall 'flute' bowls for strong ale, and a 'firing' glass with a thick base for banging on the table during toasts.

Derby porcelain, about 1775. Many such groups, designed to be seen from all sides, were made with the dinner table in mind.

In Italy there was a highly developed tradition of elaborate table sculpture in sugar paste, which was carried to truly baroque extremes. This taste for allegorical confectionery was exported to France and Germany and, once the first great European porcelain factory at Meissen was in production, it was not long before porcelain figures supplemented the more ephemeral sugar paste. When J. J. Kaendler was modelling the Meissen porcelain Swan Service for Count von Bruhl in 1737, he was instructed to follow the advice of the confectioner of the household. This tradition was followed in England as late as 1839, when the confectioner at Wentworth Woodhouse ordered porcelain figures from the Rockingham factory to dress a dessert.

A small display of this sort impressed Parson Woodforde when he dined with the Bishop of Norwich in 1783:

'A most beautiful Artificial Garden in the Centre of the Table remained at Dinner and afterwards, it was one of the prettiest things I ever saw, about a Yard long, and about 18 Inches wide, in the middle of which was a high round Temple supported on round Pillars, the pillars were wreathed round with artificial Flowers — on one side was a Shepherdess on the other a Shepherd, several handsome Urns decorated with artificial Flowers also.'

Above: *A massive earthenware dish to hold a whole cheese on its side. The flat faces of the cheese would be vertical. By John Mare, Stoke-on-Trent, about 1800.*

Right: *Asparagus servers, to enable a portion to be lifted without making the fingers greasy. (Left) Derby porcelain, about 1770. (Right) Earthenware, about 1790.*

Below: *Some cutlery of about 1800: (from the top) cheese scoop, butter spade, and marrow scoop (for the interior of marrow bones).*

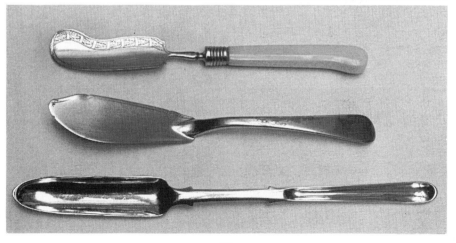

The Desert thus,

A dessert of wet and dry sweetmeats. The small circles represent individual glasses of jellies and creams (compare cover illustration). (After Charles Carter, 1730.)

A dessert mostly of candied and fresh fruit. (From Massialot, 1702.)

THE DESSERT

After dinner in the seventeenth century a selection of sugared delicacies was served in a separate place. This was a banquet, a word whose meaning has changed in more recent times. The word is derived from *bancs*, either the benches or the bench-like boards set on trestles to form a table. It was already in use in its modern sense of a grand feast in the sixteenth century but developed a parallel, more specialised meaning of a luxurious course of sweetmeats served after dinner. Once 'dessert' took over this function in the eighteenth century, this meaning of 'banquet' was largely forgotten. Sugar was an exotic and expensive import, a symbol of luxury, and the banquet provided an opportunity to show off the resources of one's hospitality in using it. The dessert of the eighteenth century was descended from the banquet. The word derives from *desservir*, meaning to unserve or clear away the dinner, because dessert was regarded as separate from the dinner

proper and might be served elsewhere. With the serious eating over, visual fantasy could be given free rein.

The hour of dinner became gradually later, from about two o'clock at the beginning of the century to six o'clock at the end. Because dessert came at the end of the meal, candlelight played a more important part in its display than it did in the main courses. This accounts for the use of glass for dessert. A plateau of mirror-glass in the centre of the table reflected light from the candles on to the figures and other decorations placed on it. When Lady Grisell Baillie dined with Lord Mountjoy in 1727 she was impressed by the row of glass 'pyramids'. Hannah Glasse in the *Compleat Confectioner* (1762) explains the arrangement:

'A high pyramid of one salver above another, the bottom one large, the next smaller, the top one less; these salvers are to be fill'd with all kinds of wet and dry

19

A set of shell dishes, suitable for dry sweetmeats. Bow porcelain, about 1755.

A core mould for a pyramid of jelly. The painted design would be seen through the jelly. Creamware, about 1780.

sweet-meats in glass, baskets or little plates, colour'd jellies, creams &c. biscuits, crisp'd almonds and little knicknacks, and bottles of flowers prettily intermix'd, the little top salver must have a large preserv'd Fruit in it.' (See cover illustration.)

Recipes for jelly exploited the qualities of glass. Elizabeth Smith's recipe for ribbon jelly (1753) involved running different colours into glasses in stripes. Parson Woodforde saw a pottery core mould at the squire's table in Weston House in 1782: 'a very pretty pyramid of Jelly..., a Landscape appearing through the Jelly, a new device and brought from London.'

The first English porcelains for dessert were often made in fanciful shapes. In the Chelsea sale of 1755 was 'a compleat service for a desart, consisting of a large cabbage leaf and bason, two vine leav'd dishes, two double leav'd dishes, and four small sunflower leaves', as well as vessels in the form of partridges, melons and cauliflowers. The idea of a standard number or type of vessels emerged only gradually. By 1780 there was a 'typical' service, consisting of a tall centre dish, twelve serving

Fanciful shapes became the norm for dessert serving dishes. Bow porcelain, about 1760.

The centre dish in a dessert service stood on a tall foot. Porcelain by Charles Bourne, Stoke-on-Trent, about 1830.

Above: *A pair of pierced baskets for fruit. Creamware, about 1770.*

Below: *A pair of glaciers for ice-cream, with liners and covers. Derby porcelain, about 1820.*

Below: *Cups for custards or creams. Worcester porcelain painted in the London workshop of James Giles, about 1770.*

dishes (four each of three different shapes), a pair of tureens for cream and sugar, with covers and stands, and 24 plates. The twelve serving dishes were usually known as compotiers and from about the 1820s began to be raised up on a foot like the centre dish.

To the basic service might be added pierced baskets, shell dishes and glaciers with liners for holding ice-cream or chilled fruit. These can be readily distinguished from the ice pails for cooling wine bottles because glaciers also have covers. The tradition of baskets for dessert led to the use of piercing for the edges of dessert plates and the covers of cream and sugar tureens.

Porcelain figures were made specially for dessert. Chelsea in 1755 sold 'six beautiful small figures, love in disguise, for desart', that is, a set of Cupids in fancy dress. Cups, often with a handle and a cover, were variously known as custard cups or cream pots. Their size may seem small, but recipes for custards and ice-creams consisted mostly of cream, the main difference between them being one of temperature.

Above: *The pierced edge indicates use for dessert. Creamware, about 1770.*

Below: *A wine cooler for a bottle. Silver, 1820.*

23

A decanter of about 1820, with a silver bottle ticket to identify its contents. It sits in a coaster, to be pushed around the table once the cloth is taken off.

Once dessert was served and the servants withdrew, the serious drinking began. After a glass or two the ladies retired to make tea in the drawing-room. The men were supposed to join them once the tea was made, but in practice the interval was extended and its purpose usurped for the sake of male conviviality and heavy drinking. Madame de Bocage reported:

'After the dessert, especially in the country, the cloth is taken away and the women retire. The table is of fine Indian wood, and very smooth, little round vessels called coasters ... serve to hold the bottles, and the guests can put them round as they think proper. The name of each sort of wine is engraved on a silver label attached to the neck of the bottle; the guests choose the liquor which they prefer and drink it with as serious an air as if they were doing penance, at the same time drinking the healths of eminent persons and fashionable beauties. This they call toasting.'

Coasters and bottle tickets enabled the company to dispense with servants in order to gain privacy, to speak their minds and behave appallingly if they felt like it.

Derby biscuit (that is, unglazed) porcelain. The factory advertised biscuit figures for dessert in 1773.

24

Dinner 'à la russe', about 1880. The dishes of food have vanished, and the cutlery and glasses have multiplied. The centrepiece sits on a platform of mirror-glass.

VICTORIAN REVOLUTION

The traditional way of serving a formal dinner sacrificed convenience to good looks. Each massive course took the cook half an hour to dish up and then sat cooling magnificently on the table for another hour before much of it came to be eaten. If one wanted something from the many dishes not within reach, one had to ask across the table or catch the attention of a servant. It is not surprising that it became good manners not to sample more than two or three main dishes in each course. E. Hewlett noted: 'if there are not many to attend on the company, it is probable that things will be asked for several times before all can be served; and if there are many servants they may be running one against the other, and spilling the sauces etc. on the company, the table cloth or the carpet.' Thomas Walker in 1835 pronounced: 'The only convenient plan is to have everything actually upon the table that is wanted at the same time, and nothing else.'

The solution was a form of production-line service, not inappropriate for the first factory age. It is the system still used for formal dinners today. As early as 1807 it was noted that 'in some houses one dish at a time is sent up with the vegetables and sauces proper to it; and this in succession, hot and hot.' Not until the 1850s did this system become common, named *à la russe* because it was said to have been introduced by the Russian ambassador to the court of Napoleon. Each dish was carried round the table by servants to each diner in turn, serving from the left. Dishes too heavy to carry round, like roasts, were first presented and then taken to a side table for carving. According to Mrs Beeton:

'The table is laid out with plate and glasses, and ornamented with flowers, the dessert only being placed on the table, the dinner itself being placed on the sideboard, and handed round in succession, in courses of soup, fish, entrées, game and sweets. This

25

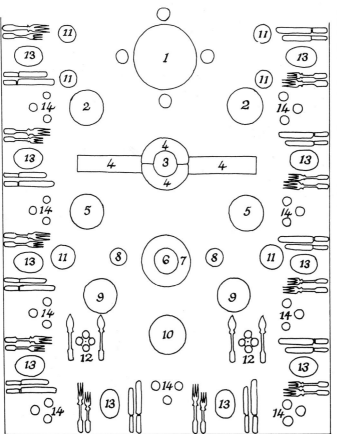

Dinner 'à la russe'. A table as far as the centrepiece (1 on the plan), a vase of flowers surrounded by china shells; 2, china figures supporting glass dishes of fruit; 3, candelabra; 4, glass troughs containing cut flowers; 5, 9, china dishes of fruit; 6, 7, glass water jug on velvet stand; 8, glass water goblets; 10, plant in china vase; 11, water carafes; 12, small cruets; 13, napkins, with a bread roll in each; 14, sherry, claret and champagne glasses. (After Walsh, 1879.)

is not only elegant but economical, as fewer dishes are required, the symmetry of the table being made up with the ornaments and dessert. The various dishes are also handed round when hot; but it involves additional and superior attendance, as the wines are also handed round; and unless the servants are active and intelligent, many blunders are likely to be made.'

Critics complained that dinner now took four hours instead of two and a half or three as before. Since the servants were engaged in the continuous production of food and drink, each diner had to have four knives and forks and four wineglasses at their place setting before the meal began. Mrs Beeton was afraid that service *à la russe* required more cutlery and crockery than most of her middle-class readers would have. The tradition that dessert was not part of dinner meant that dessert cutlery did not have to match the rest, and this often provided the excuse for more elaborate decoration.

Already in the 1820s when two glasses were to be set by one place butlers were advised: 'if there is any difference in the size of the wineglasses, let one of each sort be put to each person ...' After about 1860 more utensils at a place setting encouraged those utensils to be differentiated. Specialised fish knives and forks came into use, followed later by the round-bowled spoon for soup. Towards the end of the century the dessert spoon and fork were sometimes placed above the place setting but were just

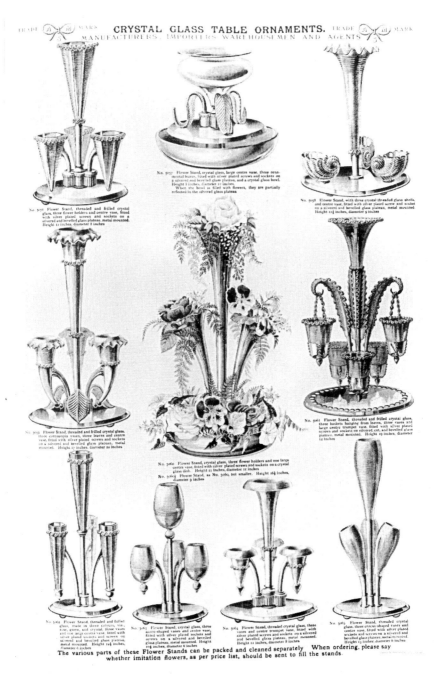

Late Victorian flower stands. Glass and flowers have triumphed for the centrepiece.

27

ENGRAVED TABLE GLASS.

Glasses for different wines become differentiated by shape. The glass service expands to compete with china in offering a range of pieces for table and dessert.

28

GROUPS OF FRUIT.

See page 274.

The fruit displayed on the table was often for show only. If the displays were hired from a confectioner, the same pineapple might reappear at several dinners.

as likely to be laid at either side, or to be brought only when dessert was served — as had always been the way before *à la russe*. Hitherto glasses of the same shape had been made in different sizes, described as for liqueur, wine, claret, hock and champagne. However, it was not until after about 1860 that manufacturers began to market glasses as matching services including all these types, with separate glasses for sherry and port. Enterprising firms extended the glass service to include a whole dessert service.

Before service *à la russe*, the art of food had been just one among many decorative arts at the table. Now the other arts were beginning to lose their traditional job of presenting the dinner. This restriction was made possible because a critical attitude to decoration arose during the same period when most food and wine ceased to appear on the table. As mechanisation enabled decorated goods to be made more cheaply for more and more people, many traditional forms of decoration became devalued in the eyes of the leaders of taste. As the reformer Henry Cole put it: 'Expensive

and intricate detail does not necessarily belong to elegance of form and design.' Decoration had to be confined to where it was strictly appropriate.

The typical heavyweight table decoration of the early nineteenth century did not pass the test. Thomas Walker in 1835 com-

A sugar-paste Viking ship filled with fruit, about 1880.

BIRD'S CUSTARD POWDER

"His Third Glass"

Numerous are the uses for **BIRD'S** Custard Powder:—Dainties in
endless variety, the choicest Dishes, and the richest Custard!

NO EGGS! NO RISK! NO TROUBLE!

*Late Victorian custard glasses in action. This
appears to be a buffet, but they also appeared
on the dessert table.*

flower stands, usually composed of trumpet-like flower holders, came into fashion and continued to be made as late as 1920.

The new and old methods of table service co-existed and modified each other. A dinner might be served in the traditional way but in a larger number of smaller courses. The last course, before cheese and dessert, would by now be a sweet course, apart perhaps from a couple of savoury dishes offered round first and then removed. Alternatively, even if all other dishes were carried round by the servants, the soup, the fish and the joint could in turn be placed at the end of the table for the host to dispense in the old way. Decanters could likewise remain on the table, alternating with water bottles at the corners. These were placed just inside the salt cellars, which at the end of the century still had to be flanked by paired table spoons in time-honoured fashion.

For servants the burdens imposed by any lavish dinner were equalled by its temptations. The footman in charge was advised: 'If you have not the opportunity of clearing away the plate, wine and fruit, as soon as the company all leave the table, lock the door, and keep the key in your pocket; or those whom you have to assist you, may help themselves, and by so doing ... render themselves unable to give you any further assistance ...'

plained: 'Intercourse is prevented as much as possible by a huge centrepiece of plate and flowers, which cuts off about one-half the company from the other, and some very awkward mistakes have taken place in consequence, from guests having made personal observations upon those who were actually seated opposite them. It seems strange that people should be invited, to be hidden from one another. Besides the centre-piece, there are usually massive [candle] branches to assist in interrupting communication.'

Mrs Beeton recommended that the table for a dinner *à la russe* should be laid with flowers and plants in fancy flowerpots down the middle, together with some of the dessert dishes. These were low enough not to impede the table talk. There was need, however, for a centrepiece that would be impressive without obstructing the view. Glass was the answer. Around 1860 glass

AFTER 1900

During the twentieth century it became normal for middle-class households to have no servants. In terms of the service at dinner parties, this did not necessarily make much difference, because occasional or part-time help could be hired. It was the democratic ideals of the century which made the difference. There were now some people who felt uncomfortable about the ostentatious presence of servants, regarding this as evidence of an old-fashioned social order. The do-it-yourself dinner encouraged the return of food to the centre of the table, although only one main dish usually sat there at any time. Cutlery and glasses for the whole meal needed to be set ready at each place setting, just as they had been in service *à la russe*.

After 1900 side plates became more common and it became popular to serve after-dinner coffee.

An even more fundamental shift in attitudes was the change from white to brown, from refined to unrefined. For centuries refinement and whiteness, both in the bread one ate and in the pottery from which one ate it, were desirable qualities indicating social refinement, separating the 'quality' from the unrefined masses. The industrial revolution of the nineteenth century made refined white bread or pots available to almost everyone. By 1900 there was a concerted intellectual reaction against modern industrial society, arguing for a move back to the land, back to small-scale production, back to a closer relationship between man and nature. Followers of William Morris and Edward Carpenter, eating wholemeal bread off brown country pottery, represented a little 'counter-culture' in opposition to the practices of mainstream Edwardian society.

Until the 1960s this 'good and simple life' did not become an everyday reality for many people rather than a holiday romance. Nevertheless it occupied a position of moral superiority from the beginning of the democratic twentieth century, even before the modernist designers stripped away ornament as useless, old-fashioned frills. Such puritanical ideas tended to inhibit fashionable society from setting its tables in ostentatiously novel ways. On the whole the late Victorian tradition was continued in a watered-down version. Following the current taste for simplicity, dinner might by 1920 be served on mats on the bare table. Its gleaming polished surface was the more impressive for not being covered with decorations. Another innovation of the earlier part of the century was the use of electric lights, which could be placed inside vases or bowls of coloured glass on the table. The resulting glowing colours made further decoration redundant.

Two modern developments point the direction for the future. One is the influence of oriental ways of serving food, involving numerous dishes on the table at once. The other is the explosion of talent in the modern decorative arts which, in a curiously old-fashioned British way, are usually referred to as the crafts. The associations of this word with homespun rusticity are quite inappropriate to the sharp and stylish work which has been produced since about 1970 and which is just beginning to be adapted in versions for mass-production.

FURTHER STUDY

The best book is L. C. Belden, *The Festive Tradition: Table Decoration and Desserts in America, 1650-1900*, W. W. Norton and Company, New York and London, 1983. It draws on a great deal of English material. The author served at the Henry Francis du Pont Winterthur Museum, Route 52, Winterthur, Delaware 19735, USA, which is perhaps the best place to see tables set with original wares in an authentic manner. In Britain similar exercises have been done, usually as temporary exhibitions: the catalogue *Pyramids of Pleasure*, from the show at Fairfax House, York, in 1990, is excellent, and see also *Country Life*, 28th June 1990. For the most part information is hidden in books and museum displays which are materials-based, on silver, glass or ceramics. R. J. Charleston, *English Glass*, George Allen and Unwin, 1984, and P. Glanville, *English Silver*, Unwin Hyman, 1987, are outstanding, as are the collections of the Victoria and Albert Museum, Cromwell Road, South Kensington, London SW7 2RL (telephone: 071-938 8500), where both authors have served. Many of the objects shown in the present work can be seen in the Castle Museum, Norwich, Norfolk NR1 3JU (telephone: 0603 222222, extension 71224).

On food see *Food and Drink in Britain*, Penguin, 1984. The author, C. Anne Wilson, organises an annual seminar at Leeds University on the history of food and society. The papers from the second seminar have been published under her editorship as *The Appetite and the Eye*, Edinburgh University Press, 1991. The Brotherton Library at Leeds University houses in its Special Collections the Preston and Blanche Leigh collections of early cookery books. Anyone requesting an appointment to consult items would be well advised to purchase the catalogues first. Prospect Books, 45 Lamont Road, London SW10 0HU, publish the journal *Petit Propos Culinaires* and facsimile editions and bibliographies of early cookery and household books. Also useful are G. Brett, *Dinner is Served*, Toronto, 1968; S. Mennell, *All Manners of Food*, Blackwell, 1985.

A chestnut basket, with a cover, and piercing only part of the way down. (After the Leeds Pottery catalogue, 1783.)